JabberWalking

Juan Felipe Herrera

CANDLEWICK PRESS

First edition 2018

Library of Congress Catalog Card Number pending
ISBN 978-1-5362-0140-6 (hardcover)
ISBN 978-0-7636-9264-3 (paperback)

17 18 19 20 21 22 LEO 10 9 8 7 6 5 4 3 2 1

Printed in Heshan, Guangdong, China

This book was typeset in Adobe Garamond Pro.

Candlewick Press
99 Dover Street
Somerville, Massachusetts 02144

visit us at www.candlewick.com

Hurry!

Jabber Notice!

Just noticed that I did not supply you with a most practical item. What is this puffy, blue-cheesy, Jabberwalking volume going to teach you? **Warning:** Do not excessively slow down, we are in a total, serious, puffy hurry. Read the following three items ASAP— in about four seconds—

The Four Jabberwalking Techniques:

1. The Art of Jabber**walking**
2. The Art of Jabberjetting (Jabberwalking inside a bonified **airplane** going a gazillion miles per hour)
3. The Art of Jabberwalking with a **Newspaper** emblazoned with moody and rock-star faces
4. The Dangerous Art of the **Period** Rebel Planet **Frijol!** And just maybe—
5. El **Dasho! (bonus)**

Disclaimer:

There are some hefty, blue-cheesy, puffy surprises on the Jabber Walker's road. Trust me. And of course, I do need to attend to Lotus's various physical needs as we Jabberwalk. After all, she is a bonified Chinese Pit Bull. Anything can happen, in particular, if a goofy dog happens to **bump** through her most guarded, precious, and scrunchy five-foot radius of private, blue-cheesy space & on occasion she does (I must admit) **love** to jump, propelled by her furry hind spud-shaped padded paws.

For all those in a hurry in this blurry,
itchy planet & all those (like me) that
cannot stand still . . . this is for you!

For Margarita Robles, my Jabberwalking partner through this magnificent life
For all my children, grand and great-grandchildren
For my Sisters, Concha and Sara
For all my families

And in memory, for my cousin and poet,
Vicente Quintana

For all my doggies once upon a time,
Rowdy
Spanky
Princess Pei-Pei
Rocko
Dusty
&
Lotus

And, as in uffish thought

The Jabberwock,

Came whiffling through

And burbled

he stood,

with eyes of flame,

the tulgey wood,

as it came!

—from *Jabberwocky*, by Lewis Carroll (1832–1898)

[The Incredible
Chapter Uno]

On the Questionable Yet True & Tried Method
of Jabberwalking in a Fast, Fast, Fast World!
(And an Unexpected Journey to the Library of
Congress across the Street from the White House!)

Wait!

[**Jabber Notebook:** Before you burble through the Tulgey Wood, let me get my stuff ready! OK? My desk at home is a total, absolute, puffy, putrid, fluffy, blue-cheesy, incandescent, forest-like mess! It's been photographed in the papers already. Jeez. My well-groomed, perfumed, blonde-reddish-colored Chinese Pit Bull Shar-Pei—*Lotus*—waits for me to take her for another walk, as usual. She is my buddy, Jabber partner girl. I am panting. She is panting. We just finished whiffling through five blocks in circles and zigzags here in Fresno-York. Getting ready to travel to Washington, D.C., for my first set of meetings as the Poet Laureate of the United States! Got to finish up washing Lotus's spud-shaped paws because she will lick them for hours and I do not want her to gobble all the creepy, creepy, creepy things hanging from her spud-pads and claws. Spring bugs are all over my tiny house, even my John Lennon glasses for my fuzzy, chocolate-colored eyes that can't see too far or too close—after all these years of Jabberwalking in the whirly world of things. Been Jabberwalking so many years my skeleton crackle-clicks at the joints and my neck crooks up and my hand bones crackle-whack. There's no stopping once you are a Jabber Walker—a bonified poet on the tangly streets of the planet where human beings breathe as best as they can and slap their hands in the air to greet the sun where periods and dashes and verbs and nouns come flying.

Fly, fly! I am putting on my flippy sombrero and my original, winged Jabber boots, got my Jabber backpack and Jabber journal for a fast, fast, fast, scribble poem-burble-on-the-run, a true burble in this light-speed tulgey world of surprising things under the wobbly sky. There will be a silvery jet waiting for me and for you, all the way to D.C. for my first Laureate visit! Come, Lotus! Let's gooo!

No matter how far I go. No matter how fast I ride the pasty, pebbley sidewalks — my Mamá Lucha and Papá Felipe come to me — somewhere in my heart life. How poor we were. The trailer we lived in made out of blonde chopped wood my father bought at the lumber shop and how he slapped it on top of a rusty, dilapidated car he found on a hill in Vista, California, in the '50s. We stopped in ranchitos to work picking grapes, lettuce, and corn. The trailer was called la trailita. Trailita. This word was not allowed at school. Or any word in Spanish . . . until I did not want to speak in Spanish anymore or even call *hello* to my mamá in Spanish as she waited for me outside of class. Does that happen to you? I wanted to cry. Silence overtook me. There was another way. Another road — to become a Jabber Walker! Yes, to listen to teachers who encouraged me like Mrs. Lelya Sampson in third grade, to step up to courage. To write and become a speaker for others. A poet with the "eyes of flame."]

Let's go! ¡Vámonos!

Slide on your Jabber Booots! Let's move and

"Let us go forth in the bold day!" As **Walt Whitman** would say—

a true, superb, and bonified,

incandescent Jabber Walker!

[The Incredible and Zoomy
Chapter Dos]

On the Question of the Questionable Instructions
for the Superb and Fine Art of Jabberwalking

You have to move **fast!**

Move, move, move—with your Jabber paper pad in arm and hand—well, most of all with your Jabber, Jabber—your burbles—whatever pours out of your bubbly burrito head down to your paper pad thing or liquid screen. Just wait . . .

Your burbles are going to become a
Seismic & Crazy Epic Poem!

It is all out here— **start walking!**

Start burbling start scribbling start throwing things— all the letters and faces dripping down on your paper rectangular pad!

But,

Remember—

You have to JABBERwalk
(that is, write & walk & write & walk nonstop on the Jabberwalking lanes—
wherever you find them—of the city).

And

Most of all . . .

You! You! You need to go, go, gooo—FAST!

much faster . . . (I have a secret.) shhh . . .

[The Unexpected and Body-Chilling
Chapter Three]

Wherein the New Jabber Walker Learns the
Blue-Cheesy, Questionable, and Life-Saving
Secret of *Where to Go*!

THE SECRET:

You do not have to know where you are going!
Or what you are saying!

(I know, yes, yes, I know — yep. This sounds ridiculous and blue-cheesy.
However, this may be better since the Poem, the burble, does not want to know
where it is going or even what it is saying. I learned this from my poetry burble,
incandescent professor, Marvin Bell, at the Iowa Writers' Workshop, University
of Iowa in Iowa City, Iowa. More or less. Seriously!)

Follow this line to get an idea of the possible route

a burble may take. Be prepared . . .

Wait!

[Jabber Notebook: Walking fast and writing fast—I love this—in an art museum or mercado in Tepic, Nayarit, in Central Mexico, land of the Huichol Indian Peoples. Love, love it—because there are a megaton of faces and voices, manikins, grimy fish on splintered stilts, atomic structures and dangling isotopes and putrid donkey smells and flashing plexiglass roof colors and **frying chicken heads** and red-green-brown-yellow-blue salsa pools on spotted stone bowls and titanium-white tubes of paint sloshing, coming straight at your burrito head!]

Where do you love to walk?
Where do you feel **megalicious** happiness?
Where do you really feel superb and super-ready and **galactically** free—you!

Hey!
Jabberscribble something about these questions now!
Get your Jabber pad (you know that bag or satchel or pack or journal or tablet that you carry while you are walking to school or when you are skating or hauling all of your organic veggies and cookies and tacos and bagels and falafels and sandwiches, kimchi and rice balls and peanut-butter tostadas and **guacamole balloons** as you rotate around the earth with all of its hairy and wet-nosed creatures).

Now . . .

move! Walk (Repeat: you have to walk to be a Jabber Walker) and scribble your burbles, amble, roam, flap your arms. . . . What I mean is that you need to pour out all the tiny electric-head-idea worms and dreamy roaches, things-you-see-and-hear worms onto your Jabber paper pad as you

look down

at your

paper

pad.

Walk-walk

forward. Please do not spill the burble worms . . .

Or

they will . . .

fly all over the place!

TIPS:

(next short chapter) ⟶ Hurry!

[The Unbelievable & Inevitable
Chapter Cuatro]

On the Odd and Unspoken, Dubious Tips
on Jabberwalking (That Is, Scribbling with Your
Tongue Flapping About and Your Muddy Hair
Poking and Mangling Your Ears & Snaking Around
Your Mud-Speckled Hair with the Likely Possibility
of Perforating Your Throbbing Brains)

TIP:

SCRIBBLE your burbles, your words of things—that you see and think and feel but it is really not thinking or even feeling. It is plain ole bonified, fuzzy, puffy, blue-cheesy, incandescent, brave

Jabber!

Jabberwalking is not for the neat, polished, well-combed aesthete—it is as stated in the epigraph by Señor Lewis Carroll at the start of this fine volume. Jabberwalking is for the Jabber Walker with **"eyes of flame."**

So:

Scribble what you see

Scribble what you hear

Scribble out the electric Jabber worms crawling out of your head & eyes

Scribble what that dude skating by is hollering

Scribble everything that goes on in the cafeteria

Scribble what all the teachers say in the halls

Scribble what your grandma is saying as she pushes out of the peso store

As she rifles through her bag of oatmeal cookies and paperbacks

by **José Antonio Burciaga!**

Scribble

(If you are Thinking . . . Just say,

"I am thinking, duh!" and pour it all out

of your . . .

BURRITO-SIZE JABBER HEAD!

There is a faster and blue-cheesy furious way—

[See next short chapter . . .]

[The Incredible and Drooling

Chapter Five]

On the Slight and Possibly Long,

Blue-Cheesy Detour of Jabberjetting

(You Are Going to Need Some Serious Chips!)

You can Jabberwalk on the gooey street
AND if you have some serious tortilla chips you can
Jabberscribble burbles nonstop in a

Jet—— going to **AnywhereLandia**

or Fresno-Jabber-York to D.C.!

In

a Jet:

You can see the raggedy clouds
  tiny tiny fields with green sprouty eyes grisly canyons
    spilled with brutal snow and scary darkness
      and cilantro leaves

I hear something . . .

Please read carefully:

In a noisy-noisy ear-blowing jet (I repeat)—

You are sitting in a cramped, nasty, blue-cheesy,
pressured, sweaty plastic seat in between two blue-cheesy,
volcanic, drippy, puffy, **human beings** like you! And
also in front and back of you there are

TWO MORE

puffy, blue-cheesy, drippy, pressure-cooked, volcanic

sweaty # humanoids!

Here is the magnificent question:
What else can a bonified Jabber Walker do
In a boxed-in cruddy and crummy situation such as this, I ask you?

Have you ever been totally, epically, mega-smashed

in between two (I repeat) **two** stinky, puffy, drippy, volcanically

sweaty, meat-gobbling, veggie-spilling, fried-chicken-
with-pesto-sauce-exploding humans—part amphibians?

There is only **ONE THING** you can do
in such a predicament . . .

(A Jabber Walker never waits to spew a burble . . . when your eyes are *of flame*,
you are always scribbling, burbling, writing—whether you are racing down the
Jabber lanes of the city or being mashed inside a jet in between two humanoids!)
Sometimes, I write for four hours, craggled and sweaty and wrinkled from, let us
say, New York to Fresno-York, California. Your hand bones are going to hurt in a
major way! Take a blue-cheesy look at one of my Jabber Jet Journal pages:

However . . .

HOWEvER—

HoW EVER . . .

HOW EV_{ER}

HOW EVERR R ——

how ever!

(Please turn this page quickly after you read the following!)

After four hours of nonstop Jabberwriting,
after four hours of moving your Jabber hand,
like a Jabber fish across your writing pad
(Or your tablet or your smartphone)
a tiny, itsy, bitsy, granola alphabet appears—

Even—if you have **misspelled** everything!
And even if you have a laptop or
an iPad of miles and miles and miles of scribbles
YOU,
YES
YOU! In four hours—will have an . . .

(what follows is indisputable!)

ALMOST-BOOK!

(a most precious Jabber BURBLE work! A work of true Jabber art scribble that can be transmogrified into a bonified, genuine, genius **Book!**)

Yes — an *almost* — BOOK!
An honest-to-goodness almost-book! And if
you are Jabberwalking, that is, moving your blue-cheesy body
across the knobby, bumpy, **bean-frijol** planet, you too will possess an
honest-to-most-goodness, long, long

Jabber

Poem burble!

However . . .

However...
(I repeat!)

there is a tiny problema!

well, a major Problema!

A Mighty Leaping, Gorilla-shaped, huge . . .

PROBLEMA!

Rush to next short chapter! **Hurry!**

[The Superb and Unforeseen
Chapter Seis]

On the Undisclosed, Unpredictable, Nefarious, Nasty, Blue-Cheesy Problema That No One Could Ever Have Thought Of!

Read this carefully:

Most likely,

(After Jabberjetting or Jabberwalking for four hours nonstop)

You will not be able

to make any sense of all of your Jabber Notes!

I must admit this, yes it is most true and bonified . . .

(This happens to me all the time. I confess. Actually, it makes me insanely happy to

think of sitting back on my emerald-green sofa in my **USA Poet Laureate Office** at

the Library of Congress [second floor, Department of Literature] with an almost-book

on my desk gazing out through the frosty window and meditating on the platinum skies

over the White House. I giggle because I know what is about to happen.)

Yes, sadly to say it is true —

all your wobbly Jabber burbles, all your burrito-headed Jabberjetting, and all

of your wild Jabberwalking will be a . . .

jumble of crazy, gooey,

blue-cheesy,

weird,

barbarous, and blasted

scribbles!

that are IMPOSSIBLE TO
READ!

in other words . . .

A Jabberjungle!

(I repeat!)
A ghastly, gooey ball of honest-to-goodness
Jabberious jungle vines!

I have another puffy secret for you
that will definitely resolve this galactic problema!

Wait!

Hurry!

We are running out of time—

hold on—the jet is landing!

See next short chapter!

The Majestic and Masterful Short
Chapter Seven]

Wherein the Puffy Secret Is Revealed Regarding
the Actual Reading (Yes!) of the Incredible,
Gooey, Blue-Cheesy, Putrid, Puffy Burbles—
While Inside a Quiet, Serene Room Leaning on
a Semi-Organized Jabber Worm–Infested Desk
of the Burrito-Headed Jabber Walker!

Since you cannot clearly read,

understand, decipher, make out, define, follow all of your Jabberwalking burbles or Jabberjet poem, scribbled-up pages of burble melting all over the margins of whatever gooey, blue-cheesy, puffy media you utilized . . .

(please get ready for the real and true answer:

TOP CLASSIFIED personal Laureate of the USA secret)

Go to next page now! Hurry

Secret: Shhhh . . .

just copy
and
type
what you
can

ACTuaLLY

READ!

Any questions?

Question:

Sir, why will copying what can *actually be read* from the Jabberjungle
of scribbles help me make a poem?
Good question, Burrito Head!

Answer:
A Jabberwalking burble possesses the odd and spastic and

wild and unexplainable inner compulsion

TO Leap!

(Ask **Robert Bly,** American poet from Minnesota, or **Ko Un,**
the great Korean poet-monk, or the most famous painter-poet of Mexico,
Frida Kahlo, who wrote on paper bags!)

Reminder:

A Jabberwalking poem is not
          an essay or a novel
                    or a pamphlet or
                              a math formula or
                                        a blue-cheesy book report or

a paragraph of thoughts (although it can look like all of these) OR
a term paper on Alaskan crabs!

THE BIGGEST SECRET OF ALL:

A Jabber burble scribble poem is
not even . . .

a

typical poem!

A Jabberwalking poem, carved out by
"Eyes of flame" loves to
jump, fly, hip-hop, rock, roll, dive, scrunch,
dip, and

BE FREE

(wherever it lands) so it can loosen up your

Mind-Brains so you can

see things

you have not seen before . . . a **leaping** poem

is a poem that rockets you to a rare, raw, radical, puffy, blue-cheesy, and

incandescent . . .

rebel
planet,
an
unforeseen . . .
ORB of
thinking!

(It could be a bean-frijol or some kind of undefinable orb like **Mars** or

Pluto

in your burrito head . . .)

I have tested the Jabber burble's ability to hurtle me

into other galaxies in my Jabber Lab at home.

Just in case you are a curious, sweaty, puffy, blue-cheesy creature,

proceed to next short chapter on the fine art of
extracting a Jabber burble from your Jabber Journal. . . .

Hurry,
Hurry,

Hurry!

Jabber Notice: In the next short chapter:

You will write down . . . what you can actually read from the jungly, scribble burbles
that you have put

down on your Jabber pad after they leaped
out of your **burrito head** as you were skating (better to walk)
over the sidewalks of the planet at breakneck speed (I do
not recommend breakneck speed) physically undulating, eyeball rolling,
knee swiveling, **hip-hopping** (I recommend hip-hopping)
in vertebral contortions (or in a Jabber jet of puffy, sweaty, super-
squeezed sweatiness and humanoid isolation) the burbles crashing and
exploding and fizzing over each other!

Do you feel totally, epically, rushed, squeezed between things
Between puffy, blue-cheesy, sweaty, human beings all around you
Like you cannot even move your **eyes**
Like all you have available are your hand bones
Like everything else is knotted tight, like with **robotic** commands
Like you need to spill yourself out in one way or another?

If you answered yes to **one** of these . . . then

45

You must absolutely **rush** to the next short chapter!

(**Free** USA Laureate Jabber Pad Burble **Sample!**)

[The Miraculous and Most Anticipated
Chapter Ocho]

On the Questionable and Mysterious and Almost-Magical Art of Writing Down Your Jabber Burbles *(Alert: You Will Need a Sample of Your Jabberwalking Scribbles)*

Here are my recent Jabber burbles as I Jabberwalked through the Fresno-York mall this morning.

(Can you identify three to five READABLE burble words?)

ONCE &
SOMETIMES ALWAYS i THINK WHERE
IS HAPPINNESS IS IT INSIDE
A SKELETON THAT HOLDS ME
2GETHER & PUSHES EACH STEP
i PEER THRU THE WINDOW SPRING
COME NOW i CANNOT WAIT TOO YOUNG
TOO OLD PERFUME & NO WAGES
iT RAINS EVERYWHERE WHEN YOU
WANT TO RUN YELLOW GREEN &
SUPER PINK & BLACK ROAST COFFEE
DIAMONDS DIAMONDS DIAMONDS
& A FEW BALLOONS & WARS
iT IS 6 IN THE EVENING OR 5 IN
THE AFTERNOON SLEEPY SHOES
& A STRAWBERRY MALT AFTER
SCHOOL WITH BELLA MY FRIEND
FAKE NEWS REAL NEWS NO TALK
THIS MORNING ANOTHER BOMB ◎
i WANT PEACE PEOPLE RUNNING
PEOPLE LAUGHING ME TOO A LITTLE

48

Please enter Identified Jabber burbles on your Jabber Device or Medium or Towel—
(OK, here are mine.)

Skeleton

Once

Always

On the window

Perfume

Wages

& yellow rain

Roast coffee

                                                          Balloons

Diamonds

Five

Shoes

A **strawberry** malt

                                              another bomb

This morning

People running   safe

Ready for the Burble Magic?

Give your burbles **SHAPE** (simply move the words around into **fun groups**):

Skeleton

Once   always

On the window

Perfume   wages

& yellow.   rain

                    balloons

& diamonds

today

        five

                shoes

                a strawberry malt

                        this morning

People running   safe

You can also hammer out a new shape with a fuzzy sprinkle
of the words from your burble journal:

                & yellow rain
              balloons & diamonds

today five shoes a strawberry malt

                                this

      morning

Your turn.

Enter readable Jabber burbles on your Jabber Pad with

SHAPE!

Hurry! Oh!

Lotus! Where are you going? (Now what?
She's such a jumpy escape artist) . . . hey, wait!

Lotus, come here!

Lotus!
Get over here!

Listen to meee!

Please?

Lotus!

Good, Lotus. You had me . . . all worried!

Where was I?

Oh yeah . . . Next short chapter.

If you have reached this page
it means that you are advancing on
the bonified path of the Jabber Walker!

If you have trekked this far — then
you are equipped to
take on the
fine art

of Jabberwalking
beyond streets and jets
and taking on

a most

blue-cheesy form —

Jabberwalking

on the almost-magical surface

of

a

small sheet of a
bonified and day-to-day stained blue-cheesy, sweaty
& puffy, grumbly

NEWSPAPER!
A Bonified Periódico!

See next short chapter for Jabber Newspaper Periódico details—

with a guest appearance of a **handsome type** of guy

that you are going to absolutely **detest** or

LOVE

with all of your purple, shiny guts!

Hurry!

[The Mind-Boggling and Gut-Jiggling Short Chapter Nine]

On the Questionable Demonstration of
the Ways in Which a Jabber Walker Burbler
Loves & Admires & Becomes a Fan of the
Stinky, Blue-Cheesy, Puffy, and Fuzzy Thing
Called and Designated a Typical, Ordinary
NEWSPAPER! (With the Appearance of an
Infamous Middle-School Celebrity—Near You!)

Wait!

[Jabber Notebook: My father, Felipe, read newspapers in his room, which was the bedroom. 1964, San Diego, California — you could see him from the living room, which was a TV and sofa where I slept and a tiny desk for my elbows where one day I drew my hand with an ink pen with a tip in the shape of an ant — the ant pointed toward my papá reading a dark book. It was a Bible. A little further was the kitchen where I flipped a whole white-yellow plate of ham and eggs and fried pasty potatoes on the floor. A step or two further was the humongous tub and the shrimpy toilet. Pouring lethal photographic chemicals into the wide tub mouth to develop rolls of thirty-five-millimeter *black-and-white* still Yashica camera film was my favorite thing. Dry the film, expose it for a second with a light bulb while the light is off — that's how I did it. Film, photos, any kind of image on paper was my creepy, goopy world. It sparked my brains ever since my mamá showed me her mega photo album with black & whites from the 1800s! That album with a bloody-red cover was my very own personal library. That's all I had — for an only child always on the move — I guess it kinda gave me a place to find friendly faces that looked back at me, like poems. The eyes, lips, and bodies came alive when Mamá Lucha held them up to me with her voice of stories. One story is about my father's great escape! He had been mistreated by his stepmother, so rather than hang around the ranchito in Chihuahua, Mexico, he decided to jam as fast as he could and leap on the last rusty train heading to the USA.

Here's a photo of him in 1904, with his pal José Barrera. If you peel your eye-balls, you can see that he wrote on the bottom of the photograph — *Feli Herrera, October 15, 1904.* You see? From that day on, wherever he went, as a cowboy, ranch hand in Denver, Colorado, or farmworker in California, he put words on paper and newspapers! He wanted to make sure he could stop time and space, write history in a split second, even though he never went to school like yours or mine. Papá was a bonified Jabberwalker!]

Do you have writing paper at home?

Where do you keep your images? Photos?

Do you remember a family story?

How far back in time do your familia stories take you?

Oh!

I

Forgot!

We have to get going. **Hurry!**

¡Vámonos! (gotta catch a jet!)

Hurry!

Time is

totally running

o   ut!

Wait!

What on earth is this?

Is it on earth?

Where did these things come from?

Now what?

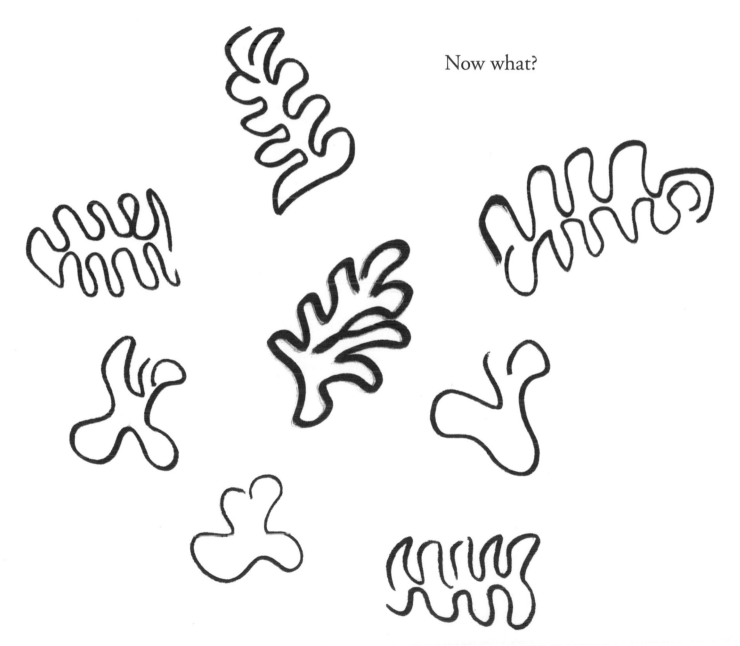

Something
is terribly wrong!
Jeez . . .

Please turn the page very slowly . . .   please.

Whew!

That was close! Ahhh . . .
Whatever that was . . . It is over!

ok, ok.

Let's get back to where we were headed . . . Uh

oh yeah . . . Let's get back to the Jabberwalking burbles on

the face of a Newspaper. Oh, and the handsome type dude

that you are going to **absolutely hate** . . . (or love, but I do not think so)

. . . here we go . . .

Oh, Oh.

Question:

Sir, what's so special about ONE blue-cheesy, putrid, fuzzy, sweaty, puffy sheet of newspaper?

Answer:

Hurry, Burrito Head! We do not have time for such a long-winded question.

(See next page for answer!)

Answer:

A newspaper

ALREADY

HAS

WORDs

On it! (ahaaaaa!)

AND

FACES . . .

**WITH EYES PEERING
INTO YOUR BRAINS
& LIPS SPITTING OUT AT
YOU WITH**

LOVE (or a putrid
tongue waggling at you!)

FOR EXAMPLE . . . see next short chapter for a sample of a
sheet from one of the most prestigious newspapers in the USA. . . .

Stop!

Stop!
Stop!

Absolutely stop!

OK—

Come on spit it out!

It is time to spit it out because all of us here
will not
be

able to
continue . . .

It is time to spit it out, really . . .

Read the following *very* carefully:

If you are having creepy, creepy, crummy doubts about this Jabber Walking thing (usually encountered while on the journey of becoming a masterful Jabberwalker of burbles) then, please proceed and take the carefully designed . . .

Sweaty
Aching
Test!

READ CAREFULLY!

HURRY!
I
ONLY
HAVE A FEW MINUTES
OR MY PLANE WILL blast directly
to the Library of Congress!

PLEASE don't just sit there with a burrito in your **ear** or I will miss my meetings!

YOU HAVE Seven Seconds!

CHECK ALL SECTIONS THAT APPLY—THANK YOU! GRACIAS! Hurry!

S.   AT.

1. This totally stinks!

2. I totally stink!

3. I am lusting for a well-shaped burrito!

4. This isn't going anywhere, seriously.

5. This is too easy, some kind of Laureate put this mess together?

6. I paid some serious chips for this!

7. I'd rather be playing my favorite video game called *Papas Fritas' Throne!*

8. I am totally lost! This is a major sham!

9. I already know how to write poetry.

10. Who cares about poetry? It is a mega-epic waste of my time!

11. I can't spell *Papas Fritas,* help!

12. Where's the principal? Ban this book!

13. What do I get out of this?

14. I want to see blood and zombies and things falling apart into edible morsels.

15. Vomit you! I don't like fun stuff.

16. I want to chill it with my homies.

17. Babe, I got what it takes already.

18. Give me some chocolate and a fried animal in a bun! Now!

19. I want to tear this thing up so I can LOL!

20. Kill this paper, I am out of here!

Well . . .

I guess I have to tell you . . .

it is crummy, boring— **& creepy**

to write—to have "eyes of flame," to burble . . .
sometimes crummier than a dead cookie in the middle of the street being
run over by a cable car on Powell Street in San Francisco where my cousin
Tito worked. I don't know what to say . . . how about a burble for you, a
kinda Jabber Walker parting gift—it is called . . .

TO BE A JABBER WALKER
      —to be a Jabber Walker
it takes
many walks alone—unnoticed
on a sidewalk you have never walked
or with friends
that come and go
it takes staring through your window at night
wondering about everything and hoping
to feel something—a something that
you do not have words for
and you just wish you did

so you

get up the next day not knowing how
you got there
and you start walking to the places
where you usually walk almost (invisible)
and you say to yourself

everything looks the same (again)
where am I going I don't know
don't even think I care but I kinda do
so you stare and stare out the window (again)

and you walk again
into the day's new light again and you breathe
and you kinda hear your breath (even if you had
a fight with your brother
in the principal's office because you
thought
he said
something about you

on
FB)

you feel your heart
it is beating

it is small

        as a sparrow
        it is as

        alive
        and

        that
        is

        good
kinda
so
you reach for a pen and a piece of paper
and you scribble something about
yourself
something real (maybe about wanting to scream
for no reason
at all)

that just happened to spill
out of your pen
that is
when you start out

on your jabberwalking road
with your
eyes

    on

        fi

          re

and
    it
    is not
crummy

any

          more.

Guess that's it — time to go.

Wait!

[**Jabber Notebook:** Someone is knocking on my door. 12:37 a.m. in the dead of night. Eleventh and C Street, San Diego, California. Mamá Lucha opens the door, apartment number nine by the entrance to the building a few blocks downhill from San Diego High School. Shaking, closes the door, comes to me with her eyes brimming with tears. Hugs me. "Your papá passed away," she says. Papá Felipe who battled diabetes, who walked downtown to La Plazita every morning and sat with his friends like Mr. Kelly and chatted about his early days as a cowhand in Denver, Cheyenne, and the big open country, who worked on railroads and water wells, highways and plows, who helped build tiny towns in southern New Mexico, who brought me yellow Ts with buffalo prints, a jackknife signed by Fess Parker, the actor who played Daniel Boone, my papá who made shoes out of pieces of leather he found on the trails, who hammered our house together with yellowish planks of wood, who chopped off the top of a car he found buried in a hill and turned all of it into our house, who always said, "Time to move, there's a new sky waiting for us, new water, new roads." Mamá and I hug in the mid of midnight. "Papá is gone. We must fight and not give up," Mamá says. "We must be kind like him, we must find happiness in all things, like rain and clouds and books—we must be friendly to all, like him too, we . . ." Mamá stops and puts her head on my shoulder. From that day on, I had to start over. I did not know what to say, what to do. All I could do was walk downtown on Saturdays like Papá and notice the clouds up there in the autumn sky—were they the same clouds? Leaves tumbled past me. Leaves, leaves. Walking, walking—walking calmed me, walking bathed me with morning light. When I got home, I picked up my six-string Stella and sat on my sofa bed and strummed the strings. Every note was a little smile from far away.]

[The Magnanimous and Mighty
Chapter Diez]

On the Highly Dubious and Questionable
Example of Jabberwriting on the Top Surface
of a Gooey, Slimy, Lead-Full, Newspaper Periódico
Sheet of Paper and Other Puffy Artifacts

Wait!

[**Jabber Notebook:** In San Francisco, about 1961, in Low Sixth (that's how schools divided grades. Low and High) I was near the door in Mr. Robert Sayden's class. Hanging out with Alfredo Aquino and Honolulu Bautista, Bobby Ng. Pop, pop-smoosh! Opened the door. Mr. Sayden scrambled out. (He was an Army Sergeant who used to let us duke it out in the cloakroom so we could resolve our differences until we were out of breath with crooked red noses.) Out in the hall, Mr. Sayden was pressing in a kid's forehead. Blood was squirting out between Mr. Sayden's fingers. Guess the boy had been peeping through the keyhole and another blue-cheesy student kicked the door open and slammed the boy's forehead and POP-smoosh! After seeing the nurse and getting his head wrapped the boy was OK—with an apple-size gooey bump on his forehead. He bobbed over to Mr. Sayden. And thanked him. Our school hero, Mr. Sayden. He even asked me to write and direct a play on Peru. "How do I go about this, Mr. Sayden? This is the first time that I do something like this," I said. "You can do it! Work with your group!" Mr. Sayden believed in me. Just like I believe in you.]

Sample of Newspaper Periódico to follow:

Go!

JABBER TIMES

THEODORUS JUNCTION, FRESNO-YORK. VOL. 99. NO. GAZILLION + 1

Justin Blubber Loses Chile Verde Pie–Eating Championship at Shark Acne Middle School in Theodorus Bunion Junction Annual Watermelon Jubilee

It was determined that according to the town officials, Dr. Pappy McPants and MC Mamá McPot, that eighth-grader Justin Blubber, once known for his cheesy guitar antics and purple, buzzed head bones as well as his sideburns on fire and odd Salsa Hip-Hop dance style, as well as Captain of the *As We Eat* After-School Spoken Word Slam, that he gobbled seventy-six Chile Verde pies outside Governor "Slick" Behemoth James's Jubilee on S. Johnson Street and somehow had a spastic response, stopped masticating the extremely horrific mounds of the magnificent tortes infested with Sweet Tea maggot flies, and proceeded to vomit on the kind and gentle audience—cheerleaders and all. My goodness. After the ordeal, Mr. Blubber signed autographs for thousands and a few hours later had twenty-seven servings of the town's signature dish, *Bird-Egg Guacamole*, known for its milky, gooey drippings and bubbles floating up into the air. Unfortunately, Mr. Blubber spilled the dank guacamole pot on Dr. McPants's Lakers suit and was expelled from school for the rest of the semester. However, Mr. Blubber made up and offered to bring his grandma's famous Tres Leches Cake for the football Homecoming Queen Coronation of Zandunga García. Students rioted and demanded Tres Leches to be served all year long. My goodness!

Hurry!

Now it is your turn!

Copy this **piece**—a *piece* is better than a "sheet."

(A "sheet" is too organized, too clean, it reminds you and me of "school sheets" of paper.
A Jabber poem is a fast poem, remember? A wild poem. An unkempt, messy, dirty poem.
A scribble, gooey, cuckoo, sweaty, puffy, blue-cheesy, incandescent poem!)

NOW—

Scribble—a human poem! A true burble—On TOP of new humanoids   and

flying cars and screechy, scratchy, crackly clouds with dog faces,

shaggy butts, and smelly cat fuzzy ears! Got it?

SO

please

proceed

and

yank off a PIECE

of Newspaper Periódico and

WRITE ON TOP OF IT &

feel

WITH YOUR EYES of FLAME!

MC Mamá Word

According to the sideburns—Slam!

Purple chile verde: Horrific!

Cheerleaders & autographs &   gooey birds,

Unfortunately—

Tres Leches &   the semester ended.

The Queen's Coronation,

While   i

Rioted all year—my goodness!

Please go to next short chapter.

Hurry, hurry!

TIP:

You can use
the following chapter's *Jabber Girl* **blog** for another
Newspaper Periódico Jabber

burble!

The Infamous and Extraterrestrial Short

Chapter Eleven

Introducing the Absolute, Unique, and Rare Example of Your Jabberwriting on the Top Surface of a Bonified and True and Puffy Newspaper Periódico Sheet of Printed Matter — the One and Only Questionable Zandunga García *Jabber Girl* Blog!

Zandunga García Reports from Pluto!

Special Supplement from *Jabber Girl* Blog

Shark Acne Middle. Vol. 99 1/2. No. 321101325. Cafeteria Churro Spot-lite

OMG! I had just finished my pre-calculus AP test and turned in my essay on the *Treaty of Guadalupe Hidalgo* to Dr. Dedo and guess what? Those high heels and all that skating with my crush at Jalapeño Arena freaked me out so I tripped into a time-space warp right outside Dr. Torres's office—you know the dude that organizes Danzantes every Xmas (that's where I met my crush holding a puppy and I thought that was so coool). My mind went totally bonkers and down down I went—you got to believe me. After class I was going to go with my mom to Fashion Blowout and browse around for a totally floor-length leather gown for my sister Ponchi's (short for Poinsettia) quinceañera or some totally Epic Mix & Match prints. OMG. Down, down until everything exploded and sizzled me into a multicolored toothpaste tube-like thing and all of a sudden I dripped out all gooey and puffy in a blue-cheese-like cocoon. The cocoon had these weird threads with tiny one-eyed drops that turned and stared at me, hypnotized me, froze me and lifted me, kinda, and swished me onto a bubble spotlight on Pluto! I fell on my butt—it was totally embarrassing—even though there is no one for gazillions of miles. Guess what? My cell phone floated out of my jeans. My cell phone works! I think it is because of the acceleration forces and the way the fabric of time, light, space, and gravity operate. My Physics teacher Dr. Sopa explained Einstein's "Experimental Moments" and how he would freak out for a little while and get these awesome ideas, like crazy poems on the Theory of Relativity and Relationships in his hairy tostada head and it would help him figure out the way the universe spread out and how it shrunk and how it had licorice-shaped tunnels that would swallow you like enchiladas. Maybe that's what happened to me! OMG, now what? Can you hear me? Anybody? Call me! Hurry! And I don't want to be late to Fashion Blowout! And my crush, jeez! This is totally embarrassing. Here's a selfie from inside the cocoon. Oh, no—the cocoon is opening its furry lid. It has all kinds of gadgets throbbing out of it. Like a tiny wet pilot station of sorts. Got an idea! Hey! Gonna hang in here and steer it back to Earth. Mamá says **Girl Power! ¡Sí Se Puede!** Whenever I think something is impossible like when I knocked down the microphone at the quinceañera warm-ups. Yes, yes . . . I can do it! ¡Sí Se Puede! Call me! 555-999-0077. Oh, no! The lid is closing and all kinds of puffy faces like the ones on Gum Ball are glowing in the blackness what's that? My cell! It's growing a tail! It is a cell-phone anemone! Help! OMG my hair is all caught up in it! It's wrapping around my arm! It's morphing into my arm now! This . . . Hey! This is so . . . ugh . . . Embarrassing! Hey! Dr. Dedo is calling! OMG. Bet you it's about Homecoming. Guess it's time to stand up for myself. Study my Spanish III Lit notes, what am I going to do about Drama class with Mr. Badges Ellis? Better burn through space to the other side. It's a cruel universe for cool blogger girls, huh?

Circle words — words
you do not use

words you like
get the feel of Zandunga's blog and get a feel of being in

OUTER SPACE

throw

those words on

a piece

of paper & scribble
a burble
as fast as you can

as if you were

flying in between
word planets — ready?
(write it in one minute)

Finished & Freaked

Tripped &
                down, down

                        a cocoon.

Everything—my puppy, what?
Guess.

I am epic because no
fabric or light can take me—

there is only one universe
one—one-eyed idea

like me.

Alert!

I forgot to tell you! (now that you finished your writing, your burble on top of the newspaper)

Congratulations!

This is incredible! You have passed the puffy, blue-cheesy, questionable, Jabber burble poetry writing method—

Jabberwalking while writing on your wrinkled paper
Jabberwalking in a jet!

Jabberdoodling on top of a
Bonified Newspaper Periódico!

(as you

choose the words that you can actually read!)

Hurry!

The Grumbling and Most Gratifying
Chapter Doce

Wherein You Will Pick Up Your Questionable,
Dubious and Rushed, Puffy, Blue-Cheesy,
Jabber Burble Degree in Jabberwalking (About Time!)

Announcement of Jabberwalking Degree:

OH NO!

LOTUS! COME here!

Stop chasing that squirrel! I said do not chase the squirrel or

it will jump across the street and get smashed by a blue-cheesy, puffy automobile

and get its **purple-cheesy guts all squeezed out** and splattered

on the smelly, gooey, rosemary bushes!

Lotus! I said . . . Hey!

Got to get to the airport!

And my meeting at the Hispanic Division at the Library of Congress?

And my meeting in the Rare Book Division? And the Prints &

Photographs Division! And the Asian Collections and the African

American Collections, and the Manuscript Division, jeez,

not to mention the video I need to scrunch out in the Folklife Center!

It's about Woody Guthrie, the folk singer who influenced Bob Dylan

and all the indie music you have ever heard in your puffy life and

the reason why I purchased a twenty-dollar

steel-string Stella guitar!

Now what?

Lotus!

Where's a car when you need one? OMG!
A cab!

Need a cab!

There's one! **Speedy's Street Cab Company** it says.

Cab!

Wait!

[**Jabber Notebook:** Golden yellow sunburst and black top — my new twenty-dollar Stella six-string. "¡Qué bonita guitarra!" Mamá Lucha said. "When you are a little sad, play, sing, write your poems — a guitar has many notes, you have many songs, you know. Let me tell you about my guitar back when I was a young woman in El Paso, Texas. Even though your grandmother, Juanita, and I lived in 'El Segundo Barrio,' Second Ward, one of the poorest barrios in El Paso, Texas, after we crossed the border in 1918, we weren't that poor, because . . . we had hearts that could sing. Your uncle Roberto bought me a used guitar on Stanton Street, downtown. Not long after, I met your Papá Felipe who played harmonica." Much later, Mamá and I played corridos of the Mexican Revolution, and songs that we made up like the artists of the day — Tin Tan and El Charro Avitia, Cuca and Eva Aguirre, singers of the '30s who performed in the new radio station, XEJ, in Juarez, across the border. Mamá stops the story, pulls out our family bloody-red-colored album from her dresser, "Can you believe your little mother sang? See this photo? It is me dressed up in a gypsy dress, rainbow colored necklaces, ruby scarves, and diamond shiny black shoes with tacones, high heels, and a guitar! Your uncle Roberto, of course, took the photograph. Look at me leaning on a wooden fence right outside our brick apartment. To sing, to dance, to perform, that was my dream, Juanito. Los Pirrines, a comedy theater, had invited me for an audition, but women were not allowed to go out in the evening and most of all, to sing, to dress up and move their bodies onstage, to be what they wanted to be! *No puedo,* I had to tell the director. That was the way it was back in the thirties. Let me tell you, I sang as loud as I could in every corner of that tiny apartment and outside in the alley. Now it is your turn, Juan."]

Cab! Cab!

What?

One thousand dollars?

Please, can you help me catch my dog! Her name is Lotus and if you do not help me catch her she will devour all the fuzzy burnt tortilla-colored squirrels in Fresno-York because her DNA has squirrel pictures in it and by the way . . .

I don't have one thousand dollars!

How about . . . seven dollars and fifteen cents? Can you work with that, Mr. Cabby Dude?

Where's Lotus?

Where's my buddy doggy with once-upon-a-time clean spud-shaped paws? Now they are all blue-cheesy, puffy, putrid, gooey paws. Maybe Lotus is slurping on a can of sardines or a **churro.** What am I going to do? Jecz.

You ever felt helpless? (I have to get to D.C.! And you have to get your Diploma!) You ever run out of options, choices . . . and all you have is you— even though you are late for everything and you are not going to be there so you might as well be invisible, but you are not. And you talk to yourself—blah-blah-blah?

Lotus!

Where are you?

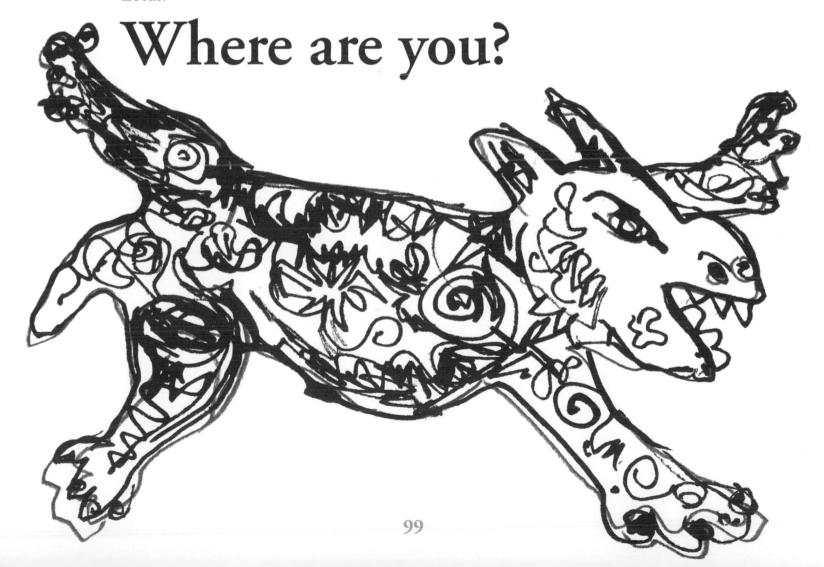

What

on

earth

are those

things floating down?

Like . . . spokes and spokes of

bicycles

splashing up

splashing down

I love autumn
with its leaves that become many different things

miniature sailboats
        on tiny oceans as the rain
rushes the edges of gutters

                away they go like incomplete letters?

What am I doing? Better get going!

Cab!

Here it comes:

Speedy's Fastest Cab in the Universe—

Hello?

Got to find my dog, sir . . .

Just don't stand there!

Step into Speedy's Cab and let's find your dog!

Hurry!

Driver:

Sir, where do you want me to drive you?

Mr. Laureate:

Just hit the pedal, Burrito Head!

Driver:

I don't understand, sir . . .

Mr. Laureate:

Look, I am running out of time! Just drive and look for a
yellow, spud-shaped-paw Shar-Pei Chinese Pit Bull
scrambling after fat, juicy, blue-cheesy squirrels.
Got that, Burrito Head?

Driver:

Yes, sir, I happen to be an expert and PhD in Dog Chaseology.
I am the only limo driver in Fresno-York licensed to . . .

Mr. Laureate:

Just hit the pedal, Burrito Head!

Driver:

I am expensive.

Mr. Laureate:

I am blue-cheesy, stinky, puffy, and unpredictable.

Driver:

No problema. Let's go!

Mr. Laureate:

Hey, you are driving two hundred miles per hour!

Driver:

You said, "Go!"

Mr. Laureate:

I am getting a very sick, green, and ugly stomach!

Driver:

How's three hundred miles per hour, sir?

Mr. Laureate:

My stomach! Stop! I'll find my dog by myself!
How much do I owe you?

Driver:

Ten thousand dollars!

Mr. Laureate:

How about a guacamole donut from
the Day of the Dead Taco Stand?

Driver:

Are you kidding? How's three hundred miles per hour?
This used to be a Batmobile!

Mr. Laureate:

Yeah sure. Aha.
Hey! Look out! Slow down!
You are going to run over all those people
crossing the street!

Driver:

Why is everyone running out of their house?
They are headed toward the Fresno-York
Supernatural Airport!

Mr. Laureate:

Hey, that's where I am going—and Lotus too! Uh . . .
They are waving signs! Can you read that?

Driver:

I am driving . . . remember?

Mr. Laureate:

SAVE ZANDUNGA GARCÍA!

They're Jabber Walkers!

Hey Justin! It's Justin Blubber!

And there's Lotus!

Lotus! My Lotus! Onstage!

Open the door!

Driver:

You owe me, Mr. Laureate! Show me the money!

Now! I have seen you on TV, you know.

Mr. Laureate:

Yeah, right, sure . . .

Lotus! My dog! My dog is out there!

We've got to save my dog and we

have to save Zandunga!

Driver:

Are you kidding me? I take cash only, by the way.

Mr. Laureate:

Save my Lotus!

Save Zandunga!

Save my Lotus !
Save Zandungaaa!

Driver:

OK, OK, OK—stop shouting! Just kidding you!
Save my ears!
How about whatever money you
have & a donut?

Mr. Laureate:

Here's seven pesos and fifteen cents—
for a donut. Come, join us!
March with us! Become a Jabber Walker!

Driver:

I am not a jabbamarcher, I am a driver . . .

Mr. Laureate:

Jabberwalking is good for your heart. And . . .
It's better than putrid donuts!

Driver:

OK. You got a point, buddy. Let's go! Hurry!

HURRY!

[The Almost-Last and Only Wiggly and Indisputable Burble Special

Chapter Thirteen]

Wherein the Most Questionable and Dubious Aspects of the Jabber Walker's Extraterrestrial Powers to Save Zandunga García are Exercised and the Miraculous U-Turn to Arrive at the Doorsteps of the Library of Congress in Time to Acquire the Most Sought After Jabber Graduation Diplomas in the Universe!

Oh, Lotus . . . I missed you. Say bye to Mr. Cabman and his Batmobile . . .

BowWOW!

Not that loud, Lotus . . . shhhh . . . my ears!

. . . Mmmmmm they smell like tuna and chocolate — I missed your blue-cheesy ears
and you licking all the creepy-crawling bugs off of your spud-shaped paws.
Most of all,
while all the autumn leaves, the burbles of the earth and sky
floated around me, I missed you being with me — yes
you and me — Jabberwalking poetry bobbin'   free
in the open air . . . and . . .

Wait!

[**Jabber Notebook:** When I jabberwalked and jabbermarched at UCLA in the late sixties, when all the students stood up for the civil rights of all, I used a legal-size yellow paper pad. The pages flapped as I crossed Westwood Ave. and passed "Margo's Carrot," the new organic food store that had the best orangey-carrot juice on the planet. My burrito head was bent down as I poured all the electric worms jazzing out crackling new ideas and words and things. All those things from my brain and body and hands led me all the way home as if I was playing a wild magnetic guitar. The strings, the notes and melodies led me and followed me all the way to my apartment on Bentley Street in Santa Monica. Once inside, I read what I could and typed what I could, then I sat back. A calm wave came over me. What was it that I said in those Jabber pages? What did those jagged letter bits do for me? Things were happening. Wars and shootings all over the place. What could my Jabberwalking do, my Jabber jottings? Things were scary, exciting, inspiring and goofy, bloody weird. How do you make sense of what's going on? Maybe my Jabber notes could bring peace to all those Jabber wigglers outside, all the young people like me, always moving here and there, trying to figure things out — here and there and there and here and sometimes never having a place to call home?]

Getting sleepy, all the walking, all the . . . Hey what's that?

A Space-Anemone Ship?

A Space-Anemone Ship?

Lotus! Get out of the pilot seat!

This is impossible!

This cannot . . . no way . . . be true!

Wait!

[**Jabber Notebook:** 1964, Mr. Headrich tells me to gawk at the painting of Salvador Dalí he flags up. Behind me Davey Alvarez pecks at my shoulder. I stare up at the smelly and dusty ancient wooden beams screeching and tilting in one thousand directions. Davey Alvarez pokes my back again then hunches over his wet, gloppy piece of paper. He is smearing his hands all over it as if they were pancakes and the paper was a giant moth-mouth that was feeding. Lean back and check out my painting buddies by the door — they are making the new fall sign for Mr. Headrich: *Welcome to art class. 10th grade.* This is the ultimate best high school in the universe! Let me get back to the subject at hand. To my right, Bob, the Englishman — he is one of the coolest friends in the world. Playing bass is his major thing — so, he is drawing guess what? Paul McCartney's bass! "Your report on Dalí is due in three seconds!" Mr. Headrich drawls at me through a five-foot megaphone on the floor next to his slide carousel — that's what it sounds like yeah. I stand up, slide to the front of the class, pop around and slap my paper on the podium. "Dalí," I say — "the man who painted dripping watches, gooey boulders, melting skies and giraffes on fire and rainbows in everything! And if you slammed your eyes on the canvases of his oil paintings you would see nothing but atomic particles! He traveled to New York, he made sofas like lips with lipstick, he drew bulls falling through space, floating legs and faces with see-through holes and atoms falling out of the sky. He wore masks and curled up his mustache as if it was two spider legs in a ballet dance! Reality was more like dream and dream more like reality!" I say this out loud with my froggy voice. Bow down — and everyone claps. Except Choo-Choo Vasquez from Logan Heights Barrio who laughs so loud he smashes Davey's bubble gum bubble. "I love Dalí, I love surrealism," Davey says and scratches the acne pyramids on his dirty, red nose and adjusts his crooked horn-rim glasses. It's the first time I have heard Davey use the word *love*. Slow-like, I shuffle back to my art desk and smear my face on my Dalí portfolio, kiss it. Turn my face — "I wish I was Dalí," I whisper to Davey. "I do not want to be cooped up in here under these rotten roof beams — I want to run and see everything melt." "Love must be like that!" He uses the "L" word again. I purr to Davey. "So, let's go! Let's be freeee!" I say. "What?" Davey drags my Stella steel-string guitar I keep under my desk. Chase him with my puffy Indian sandals. We go running as the school buzzer buzzes us out into the crazy, fuzzy, putrid blue-cheesy planet-frijol-bean that is not ever going to stop me or us and I laugh and move my mouth like a cuckoo horse that just ate a plate of extreme Cheetos. And there are tears bobbling down my cheeks. (Don't laugh!) On my eyes the diamond stuff of my soul is pouring out as if my life was made of all that — instead of being a poor brown boy, a lonesome boy, a boy who grew up in the darkness of tiny trailers and raw, raw sawdust flying up from the blue-cheesy roads up, up to a cold slick moon seeking the blue-candle light over the strange jagged mountains.]

Lotus, take those astronaut glasses off!
(you are not supposed to drive a spaceship!

You do not have a license! This does
not make sense!)

Dreaming, yes, that's it! I must be   dreaming!

Well, I do need a ride to the Library of Congress!

And you need (you guys) to get your **Jabberwalking**

Diploma, which

I happen to have in my office—let's go!

OMG!

Is that Pluto?

And that floating
cell phone &

all that . . .

tangled seaweed hair?

ZANDUNGA
Zandunga:

Do you read me? Hellooo?
          Zandunga here—

Been thinking . . . you know . . . all these planets crackling
all around me . . .

If Señor Alberto Einstein

could bend time and space — then

you and I can do it too, because

after all, it is all in your hairy head filled with

everything-formulas — like on a screen or a book

that no one has ever seen or lived — that are always . . .

What time is it? OMG!

I am going to be late to the Fashion Blowout!

WELL . . .

Come to think of it . . . now that I am out here floating around,

drifting out from all the dimensions of warps and space anemones . . .

I think I am going to write about all this in my next *Jabber Girl* blog!

You know, a fashion blowout just does not cut it . . . especially

after you read Señor Einstein and

do Danza Azteca . . .

know what I mean, after all this . . .

guess what I am going to blog about?

Hellooo . . . ?

[The For-Sure Last Horrifying &
Almost-Concluding Short
Chapter Catorce]

Wherein the Questionable Period Planet Frijol
Appears & Lotus, the Spud-Shaped-Paw Shar-Pei,
Rockets Through Black-Silver Space to Save
Zandunga García!

Stop!

Now what do we do, Lotus?

We are at a dead stop!

There's only one thing we can do, Lotus . . .

when you are at a full stop — like

facing a **Period** Planet Frijol —

like

at the end of a sentence in a poem . or —

floating like
a dash — in between things,
hear   me?

Hello, hello . . . Hello? Zandunga here . . .

D.C. **D.C.?**

Coming in for a landing . . .

—can you read me?

Wait!

[**Jabber Notebook:** Writing saved my life. What could a campesino boy raised on the way-outskirts of farm towns and cities of California do? What could I do with so many incredible things — tadpoles, newborn colts, my Papá Felipe making miracles out of pieces of ancient wood, busted metal, scuffed leather, Mamá always teaching me the alphabet from a broken book she bought for twenty-five cents at la segunda, the secondhand store — my dear traveling farm-working parents with long legs and strong hands — always on the move, making new fuzzy friends almost every week, rolling from one tiny apartment or ranch to another, slipping from one sky to another, from one deep red mountain to another. When we rumbled down the reddish-copper-colored mountains and I settled into school, I heard the poetry-like words of Martin Luther King and Dolores Huerta and Cesar Chavez, as if they were shaking hot hands with everyone they met. Those hands and words were filled with something everyone wanted ever since they were children. I was one of those children. Maybe one day I could speak like them. *Never,* I said to myself, it will never, never, never happen. **Never** — until the day came when my third-grade teacher, Mrs. Sampson, told me, *"You have a beautiful voice."* No way, it is not possible, I hushed-hushed myself. In seventh grade my music teacher asked me *"What are you?"* "Mexican!" No, that word with those two super-tall mountainy peaks on the first letter did not show itself, no one heard it, it did not pour out of my mouth! My voice was hiding in a cave in that lonesome mountain. From that day on I decided never-never to be afraid of speaking the truth—*speaking up* became my life's mission, from eighth grade to *forever-here.* Choir, almost-breathing, standing wobbly in front of others, almost-singing squeaking out my out-of-tune voice in front of others, plopping my feet on stages, nervous yet brave, I walked forward, I took steps, I picked up my guitar, I wrote, even though I did not know what a writer was or what made writing happen, it did not matter to me. Just leaned-leaned forward, moving forward-forward, like Mamá and Papá. Wrote so much, sang so much, that one day I began to write as I was walking. Day after day until I noticed that writing was like everything else—being with people, in front of everyone in as many ways as possible, jabberwalking with the world on the spinning planet. Jabberwalking was made of—kindness, I discovered. To walk and speak for the lives of others became my deeper mission like Martin Luther King, like Cesar Chavez and Dolores Huerta. A Jabber Walker writer walks to give herself and himself away like autumn leaves give away their colors and themselves to the winds, to people, each and everyone—to little animals too, to everything—to make all life so beautiful your heart becomes a diamond-galaxy that shines out fast flickering, moving, turning on lights—everywhere.]

Can

    you

         see

                me?

The Very Last

Chapter Fifteen]

Wherein an Unforeseen Event Takes Place
in the Jabberwalking Space-Time Continuum
That Changes Everything

Lotus! Hear me?

We missed the plane . . . jeez . . .

I am so sorry.

No Diplomas, I guess.

Let's head back home. Jeez . . .

Where are we?

Looks like a crazy park with **spirals** on the roofs. Maybe
we made a wrong turn into
an amusement park   or something.

Excuse me, uh . . . **Hello?**

Student: Hellooo, oh! I know who you two are!! You are the Laureate! Hey guys!

Laureate: What?

Student: And you are Lotus! What a pretty, puffy, puffy, stinky doggy!

Laureate: Stinky? What's going on here? Who are you?

Student: Jabber Girl! It's me! Zandunga García! From Bunion Junction! Don't you recognize me! You wrote about me. Now, I must say, I am the most popular girl at Shark Acne Middle School!

Laureate: Uh, Jabber Girl? And these . . . uh . . . these wild people following you?

Zandunga: Shark Acne Middle School! The superbly best Jabber Walkers!

Laureate: I am feeling green. This is weird.

Zandunga: We came to get our Jabberwalking Diplomas at the Library of Congress! Like you said!

Laureate: This is not making sense! Excuse me, can you give me a moment?

Student: See that blue-green dome right there in front of you, sir? Right there in front of your chocolate-colored eyes!

Laureate: Uh, yeah—oh! Sure . . . Oh! OH! **OHHHHHH!**

Student: It's the Library of Congress!

Laureate: OMG!—wait! That's not the Library of Congress!

Zandunga: Yes it is . . . I saw it from Pluto!

Laureate: Let's get real . . . this is not Washington, D.C.! I am sorry . . . Zandunga . . .

Student: How do you know, sir?

Laureate: Who are you? Uh, wait—you look familiar . . . you are . . .

Student: The champ! You know . . . "Tea Maggots"?

Laureate: Justin?

Justin: Correcto! Maybe you need an awesome slice of Tres Leches cake! Got some in my unique backpack made for many an edible item . . . right here . . .

Laureate: It's no use . . . I know exactly where we are . . . it's, it's. It's . . .

my . . . house! Huh, Lotus?

What on earth is going on? Can someone here explain it to meeeee? What on earth or Pluto is going on **here!**

Zandunga: Mr. Laureate, if I may . . . Einstein said, in his Theory of Relativity and New Relationships, you know, things happen faster than they appear. Things bend in space, and come together like goofy, yogurt pretzels and . . . and when you think and write at mega-speed you get places faster and stranger than you can imagine—

Laureate: How's that, uh . . . ? Pretzels?

Zandunga: It's OK . . . I'll explain later, I promise. Hey guys wait for meee!

Laureate: Guess I forgot . . . you are never alone when you are a Jabber Walker. Come back here! Lotus! You, come back here!

Zandunga: Come on, Mr. Laureate!

There are burbles to write!
There are Jabber Walkers to
meet in Fresno-York!
There are Jabber Jetters to greet!

Laureate: What about the . . .   Diplomas in D.C.?

Zandunga: I got to Pluto, remember?

Laureate: I, uh, think so . . .

You can't stop
      a Jabber Walker
         from leapin' to
            the flamey

Stars!

and return
with a burrito
head full of

incandescentSparkles!

Theodorus Bunion's
Jabber Walker
Supply Market

99 Chile Relleno Square, Fresno-York

Jabber Boot Special: 5 Pesos
(Free Shark Acne Gel Squeegee)